INVEST WITH THE BEST:
A TEENAGE GUIDE TO SMART INVESTING

Copyright © Jared Friedberg 2015

23 Skyview Drive
Armonk, NY 10504

Some images were attained from the public domain. Book design by Adam Robinson. Cover design by T.Anji.

All rights reserved. No part of this publication may be reproduced, distributed, or transmitted in any form or by any means, including photocopying, recording, or other electronic or mechanical methods, without the prior written permission of the publisher, except in the case of brief quotations embodied in critical reviews and certain other noncommercial uses permitted by copyright law.

I dedicate this book to Bruce Friedberg, my father, for introducing me to the finance world at a young age.

CONTENTS

INTRODUCTION   3

What are stock exchanges?
How are companies chosen to be part of a stock exchange?
How do stock exchanges work?
NYSE
AMEX
NASDAQ

STEP 1: PERFORM RESEARCH   8

How do you know which stocks to invest in?
P/E ratio or *Price-Earnings ratio*
EPS or *Earnings per Share*
Dividend Yield
Market Cap or *Market Capitalization*
Market Categories
Ticker Symbol
What determines the rise and fall in stock value?

STEP 2: HOW TO PURCHASE STOCKS   15

How to begin investing in stocks
Setting up an account

What strategies should you use when buying stocks?
Diversification
Holding on to a stock
How to place an order
Market order
Limit order

STEP 3: FOLLOW YOUR STOCKS' PERFORMANCE   20

How should you keep up with the performance of your stocks?
In depth check-in on your stocks
Tracking quarterly earnings
Why is it important to keep track of your stocks?

GLOSSARY   23

REFERENCES   25

INVEST WITH THE BEST:
A TEENAGE GUIDE TO SMART INVESTING

By Jared Friedberg

INTRODUCTION

Investing in stocks at a young age can be a lot of fun, although before you begin to learn how to invest, you have to understand the basic idea of what a stock is as well as where stocks are traded.

It will be very helpful to have an understanding of the different stock markets and how they work. When I first became interested in stocks I knew nothing about the different **stock exchanges**. My father sat down with me to show me a few basic facts and immediately I was hooked. I wanted to begin investing because I was so fascinated by the idea of being able to own a part of any of my favorite **public companies**. Think of learning to invest in stocks as creating a building; you need a strong foundation to get started. This introduction will show you the basic facts about how stock exchanges work and some of the history behind them.

What are stock exchanges?

When stock exchanges were introduced to the public, brokers would go to different markets where they could buy and sell stocks. These markets were crazy places to trade as there were many people yelling and screaming out prices as they increased or decreased. Today, most stock trading is done online, yet the physical stock markets still exist and people still go there to buy and sell stocks. There are many different stock exchanges around the world. In the

United States, there are three major stock exchanges. These three are the New York Stock Exchange (NYSE), the American Stock Exchange (AMEX), and the National Association of Securities Dealers Automated Quotation (NASDAQ).

Wall Street is a very famous street in the financial district of New York City. It is currently home to the largest stock exchange in the world, the NYSE.

How are companies chosen to be part of a stock exchange?

Before a company's stock can be listed, or traded, on an exchange, the company must meet some requirements called **listing standards**. These listing standards are determined by the people who run each stock exchange. To be listed on an exchange so that its shares can be traded, a company must have a minimum of the following: 1) amount of **assets, 2) earnings**, 3) number of shares of the company that will be traded each month, and 4) number of different people or companies that own **shares** of that company's stock, called **shareholders**.

In addition to all the requirements above, in order for a company to be listed on the NYSE they must pay an annual fee.

Even though the number of requirements a company must meet before being allowed to list their stock for trading on the exchange might seem kind of silly, the people who run each stock exchange have good reasons for insisting on them.

The requirements help make sure that all stock sold on the exchange is from companies that can initially satisfy and establish minimum standards of financial strength.

Since the year 1953, the stock exchange bell rings to signal the opening of the market at 9:30 am and it rings again at the closing of the market at 4:00 pm. In between those hours is where the magic happens!

How do stock exchanges work?

Basically, companies can decide to "go public". To go public is exactly what it sounds like. It allows the public to invest in the company by buying its shares. A company needs to meet certain requirements before this can happen. When those requirements are met, the company can come out with what's called an **initial public offering (IPO)**. A price (called the IPO price) is the amount that each share of the company will cost when it first goes public. Once the IPO takes place, the company becomes a part of an exchange and people can buy and sell shares of that company's stock. Companies sell shares of their stock in order to raise money.

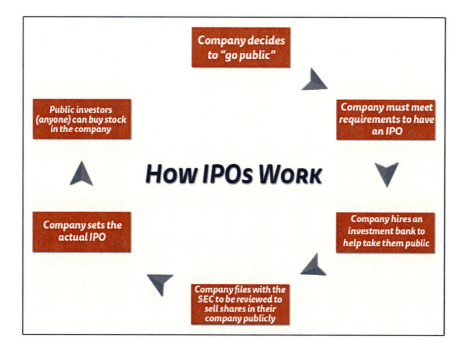

NYSE

The New York Stock Exchange is the biggest **central auction market** in the United States. It is located on Wall Street in New York City. Wall Street is perhaps the world's most famous financial area. The NYSE was founded in 1792 by several brokers who wanted to plan the best way for them to trade different **securities**. Membership was required in order to trade on the exchange. To be a member, each person had to be voted in and also had to pay for the privilege. Having membership to the exchange was called holding a seat. One had to be very wealthy to become a member. For example, one seat, in 2008, sold for $2.65 million.

AMEX

The American Stock Exchange allows for traders to buy and sell stocks on their trading floor, an area filled with monitors tracking real time stock prices, just like the NYSE. The AMEX was established in 1849 by a group of many brokers who could not afford to be apart of the NYSE. This group was originally nicknamed the "Curb" because these brokers traded stocks outside on the streets. The name eventually changed to the New York Curb Agency, and progressively outgrew trading in the street. In 1921 it was moved indoors. Today, the AMEX is known for trading **exchange traded funds (ETF's),** which are bundles of stocks that belong to the same **index**, such as technology or biotech companies.

NASDAQ

The NASDAQ was started in 1971. It was the first stock exchange to be automated and computerized. It is the world's largest electronic stock exchange and allows for people to access it from any location. The NASDAQ and the AMEX merged together in 1998, yet they still function as two separate exchanges. The NASDAQ is best known for listing technology companies, which is why I believe that this market is great for young investors like you.

This is the NASDAQ building located in Times Square. It was the world's first electronic stock market when it opened in 1971.

STEP 1: PERFORM RESEARCH

Now that you have learned a little bit about the history and basics of stock exchanges, it's time to learn how to invest! Before you actually begin to buy stocks, there is a good amount of important work to be done to insure that you are choosing good investments. You have to track information in the financial world and be on the lookout for news on different companies. There are several ways to find good reports about companies, including reading the newspaper (one of the greatest ways), researching online, and even watching TV. The reason why you have to gather information and news on companies before you invest in them is so that you know that the company is well run and is likely to have steady growth in the future. If you do not do research and just randomly pick a company to invest in, chances are you will not feel secure with your investment and may end up losing a percentage, or all, of what you invested. Throughout this chapter you will learn how to choose stocks to invest in, how to measure a stock's value, and the important terms and numbers associated with stocks.

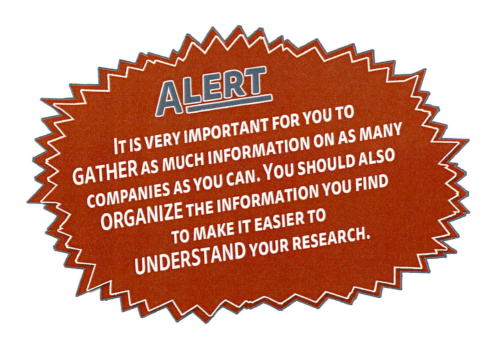

ALERT

It is very important for you to gather as much information on as many companies as you can. You should also organize the information you find to make it easier to understand your research.

How do you know which stocks to invest in?

> "Buy into a company because you want to own it, not because you want the stock to go up."
> —Warren Buffett

Since you are a young investor, you have a lot of time ahead of you. This means you do not need to invest in stocks that are very **volatile**, or unstable. You should invest in large, well-known companies such as Apple, Google and Amazon because they are very financially stable and will likely have a gradual increase over a long period of time. A good rule to follow when looking for stocks to invest in is to buy stock in companies that you like. The great thing about doing this is that you can say that you actually own a small part of your favorite company. Also, it will be easier to track and follow the news about a company that you like versus a company that you have never even heard of before. Chances are the companies that you like will usually be the ones that make your clothes, food, electronics, and other things that you need or use daily. Once you identify all the companies that you like and have heard about, you can then start to do research on which of these companies would provide the best stock value and give you the biggest *return* (money back) on your investment.

ALERT

YOU ARE A YOUNG KID! THIS MEANS YOU ARE INVESTING FOR YOUR FUTURE SO DON'T TRY TO KNOCK IT OUT OF THE PARK ON YOUR FIRST DAY. YOU SHOULD INVEST FOR THE LONG TERM.

- **WHAT ARE SOME GOOD TERMS TO KNOW WHEN RESEARCHING STOCKS?**
- **HOW DO THESE HELP DETERMINE WHICH STOCKS YOU CHOOSE TO BUY?**

These are the most important numbers you need to understand about each stock in order for you to evaluate each company's worth and if you want to invest in their stock.

P/E ratio or *Price-Earnings ratio*

This is a comparison of a company's stock price to the amount of its yearly earnings per share. For example, if a company's current stock price is $30 per share and the company earns $2 per share, then the P/E ratio is 15. This means that investors are paying $30 for every $2 dollars the company earns. This may seem like a small return, but buying the stock might be a good choice anyway. One reason purchasing the stock might be profitable despite a low P/E ratio is that low earnings in one year could precede higher growth in the company's future. However, without knowing a lot about a company, it's very hard to determine if a low P/E ratio means the company's stock is a good value. It could mean that the company is undervalued, which would make it a good stock to own; however, it could also mean that the company is actually not worth very much at all, in which case it wouldn't make for a good investment. Rather than using the P/E ratio to evaluate specific companies, it's most commonly used by investors to measure a company's value compared to other companies producing similar goods or services. We will discuss ways to compare companies below.

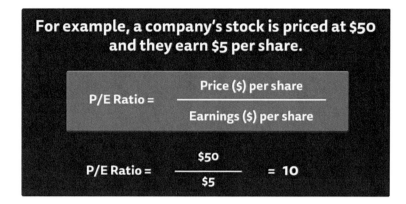

EPS or *Earnings per Share*

This is a measure of the amount of money a company earns for each share of its stock sold. It helps determine a company's profitability. Although two companies can share the same EPS, one of them will do so with less investment (also called capitalization), which means that this company used less money to earn its profit per share than the comparison company.

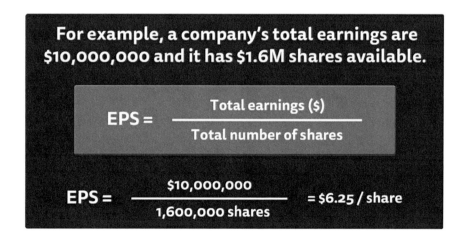

Dividend Yield

This figure can be determined by taking a company's annual dividend per share and dividing it by the price per share. It is a percentage of the dividend per share, or money, that the company gives out annually to its shareholders. Basically, this is when the company gives you free money each quarter just because you own its shares. This is an amazing thing because it is a great way to get more money back, also called *return*, on your investment.

Market Cap or *Market Capitalization*

This is the total value of all of a company's shares. A company's market cap can be calculated by multiplying the total number of the company's shares of stock by the stock's price. In general, companies with a large market cap are smarter investments. This is especially true for you because you are a long-term investor, and a large market cap often indicates that a company is financially stable and less likely to do something unexpected that might drastically change the value of its shares.

Market Categories

Sector, Industry Group, Industry - To evaluate whether a company's stock is a smart investment at its current price, it's usually a good idea to look at that company in context. This just means comparing the performance of the company you're interested in to the performance of companies that are similar. We discussed this a little bit above. To do this, you need to figure out what companies to compare to the company you're researching. Since the stock market includes companies that focus on areas from coal mining to international shipping to floral delivery and everything in between, this comparison would be hard if you had to do it on your own. Fortunately, it is made easier if you use something called a *classification system*. A classification system is just a term for a chart that tells you which other companies do what your company does. It's a shortcut so you don't have to do all the research yourself. One commonly used classification system is called the *Global Industry Classification Standard*, or *GICS*. This system divides the vast majority of publicly traded stocks into broad categories, then into less broad categories, then even less broad categories, until the category is quite specific. As noted above, the categories a stock is listed under depend on what that company does. The broadest categories are called Sectors. Each company falls into 1 of 10 Sectors; the companies in each Sector are then divided into one of 24 Industry Groups. Industry Groups are further divided into 68 industries; 154 sub-industries, and then individual companies. For instance, let's look at Apple. They are in the consumer goods sector and, more specifically, the electronic equipment industry.

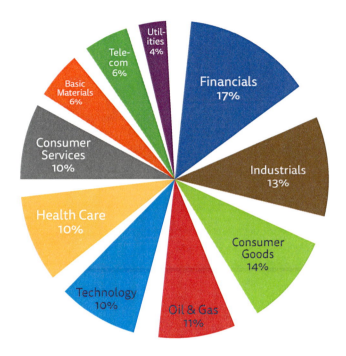

Ticker Symbol

In the stock market, each company is represented by a ticker symbol. This symbol is made up of letters. Sometimes the letters in the symbol seem obvious and sometimes they don't. For Instance, IBM is referenced by the letters IBM. Another easy one is Kraft Foods, whose ticker symbol is KRFT. The Molson Coors Brewing Company, however, is represented by the ticker symbol TAP, which doesn't reflect the company's name in any obvious way.

What determines the rise and fall in stock value?

There are several ways to measure a stock's value. Basically, the earnings per share (EPS) of a company, multiplied by its price-earnings ratio (P/E ratio), determines that company's stock price. The most basic influence on the price of a specific company's stock is the supply of its shares versus the demand for them at any given time. If there are more people who want to buy a stock than people who want to sell it, the price will go up; however, if there are more people who want to sell a stock than buy it, the price will go down. This relationship between how much of something is available (supply) and how much is wanted (demand) is a fundamental concept in the stock market and beyond, and is referred to as the *law of supply and demand*. A lot of things can influence supply and demand. For instance, if there is a rumor of good news for a company, the demand for that company's stock may increase, leading to a rise in its share price. Another important indicator of a stock's prospects is the quarterly earnings numbers the company releases. If the company beats (exceeds) its projected earnings, this will usually result in some sort of increase in the stock's price. However, if the company underperforms (earns less than predicted) for that quarter, the stock price will generally decrease.

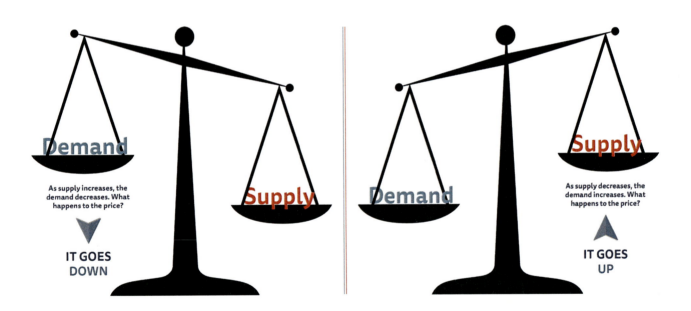

The law of supply and demand determines what the price will be.

STEP 2: HOW TO PURCHASE STOCKS

Since you are a young investor, you do not need a personal broker to manage your stock portfolio for you. Also, you should definitely talk to your parents about investing before you make any decisions to make sure they fully support you.

One time I was buying stocks in school during class on my phone and shortly after I received a call from my dad. While at work, he saw that I had placed some trades. He called to make sure that whenever I decided to buy or sell stock, I checked in with him first. It is very important that you have parental supervision while trading, as I embarrassingly learned.

As long as you take your time researching the right stocks to invest in, then investing online is the easiest and fastest way to do it. In this chapter you will learn how to begin actually investing in stock and what strategies you should consider using to help you choose which stocks to purchase.

How to begin investing in stocks

Personally, I started investing at 10 years old through an online site. My father sat down with me and helped me set up an online account with a broker. My investment funds consisted of money that I received for my birthday. I bought shares through the online brokerage site at night after the markets closed. My first stock purchase was two shares of McDonalds. The online part simply involved finding an online trading site. I began with, and still use, ShareBuilder through Capital One. There are many other investing sites such as E-Trade or Charles Schwab Online, so it's easy to find one you're comfortable using.

Setting up an account

In order to set up an account for investing, your parents must be involved and help you manage your investments. They must set up a custodial account for you if you are under the age of 18. Once they help you set up an account, it is important that they supervise all of your trades. You should talk to them first about the research you have done and let them know which stocks you are interested in buying and how much money you want to invest. They can offer useful suggestions and help you invest wisely.

ALERT

It is very important that you have your parents' permission before you begin investing. They must also help you set up a trading account online, which is very easy.

What strategies should you use when buying stocks?

Once again, since you are a young investor, you should consider buying stocks in companies that are stable because you will probably hold these shares for a long time. You are looking for companies that will have a steady increase over time and that are financially stable. Because of your age, you are probably not going to be trading stocks daily or weekly, but instead will be planning for long-term investing.

One quick word of advice I have for you is to stay way from penny stocks. These are companies that are very small, have no capital (money), and have a very low share price; literally, some can be as little as 5 cents or even less! These are not smart investments in my opinion because they can go to zero very quickly. I have experienced this before and it is not fun.

In my opinion, investing in penny stocks is like taking your money to the dump. Don't waste your time with penny stocks. They rarely take off.

Diversification

In addition to gearing your investment strategies towards the long term, it's important to *diversify*. This just means spreading your investments out over different companies, and perhaps even over different industries or sectors. It's the old "don't put all your eggs in one basket" idea. It is important that you diversify your stock portfolio and invest in different types of companies because it will lower your overall investment risk. It will help to keep your money safe from stocks and companies that may take unexpected turns.

It pays to diversify where you invest!

Holding on to a stock

Sometimes, from lack of experience, you may feel tempted to quickly sell a stock after you have bought it because it went up or down a lot. Do not let the weekly or daily shifts of stock prices scare you or excite you into selling your stocks quickly. Unless you know that something BIG is happening with the company, hold onto your stock through its price *fluctuations*, which can feel a bit like hanging on during the ups and downs of a roller coaster ride. Another very important strategy to consider when you start investing is that of setting aside your investment money from the rest of your spending money. If you do it systematically, such as through a budget, you'll stay on top of how much you've invested to date. Using a spreadsheet makes it easy to keep track of and control your investments.

Company	Ticker Symbol	Price	Dividend %	Sector	PE Ratio	EPS

How to place an order

When you have found the right stock or stocks to invest in, there are two significant things that you must consider before you place your order. The first is the number of shares of stock you want to buy; this, of course, depends to a great degree on the amount of money you are willing to spend. The second is what type of order you want to place. This is very important as it determines if you will ultimately purchase the stock and, if so, at what price. Once you have opened an account online, placing an order to purchase stocks is done through the online trading tool that you have decided to use. For this I used Sharebuilder through Capital One.

Market order

The first type of order you can place is called a *market order*. This allows you to buy the stock at the market price. This means if you buy a stock while the markets are open, you will get it at the price at which it's trading when you *execute* (place) your order. However, if you place a market order when the markets are closed, the trade will execute as soon as possible after the markets open. (I do not recommend placing a buy order after the markets have closed because the stock you want to purchase could go up after closing hours and open at a higher price than the one it closed at the previous day. This could leave you paying more than you wanted to or planned).

Limit order

The second type of order you should know about is a *limit order*. This allows you to determine the maximum price you want to pay for a certain stock. For instance, if a stock is trading at $15.50, but you only think it's a good investment if you can get it for $15, you can place a limit order to buy the stock that stipulates you will only buy the stock if its price declines to $15. This is very useful because you do not want to sit in front of the computer all day watching the stock to see if and when it gets to the price at which you want to buy. It is easier to set a limit order to get the stock at a lower price. However, if the stock you want does not drop to the limit price you set, the trade will not go through.

These are important things to consider before investing in stocks and I use these strategies when investing to help ensure that I make the right decisions.

STEP 3: FOLLOW YOUR STOCKS' PERFORMANCE

After you've invested in a stock, or multiple stocks, you cannot simply ignore the companies. Although you should, in general, buy stock and hold on to it for a long time in order to give it a chance to grow, this doesn't mean you should forget about it. It's very important after you buy stock in a company to continue to read about and research that company. This does not mean you have to read and research that company every single day you own it, but it's important to have a sense of what's happening with any company in which you've invested money.

How should you keep up with the performance of your stocks?

You can easily check the price of your stocks on a cellphone or computer. It is fast, reliable, and fun!

There are many ways to stay informed about how your stocks are doing. The simplest is to check the current price of the stock to see if it has risen or fallen, and by how much. This is something that I try to do every day. Although I recommend that you keep track of this, I encourage you not to get emotionally caught up in your stock's day-to-day performance. As I noted above, if you check the price of a stock you own one day and see that it's going down (and part of investing is understanding that this will happen at times, regardless of how carefully you've chosen the company in which you own shares), this should not automatically scare you into selling. Remember that day-to-day changes may not mean much in terms of the overall long-term growth of a company.

In depth check-in on your stocks

Although checking the price of your stock is easy, it gives very limited information about what's going on inside the company. To maintain an understanding of your investment, you should try to read as many articles and reports about the stocks you own as possible. One way I find information about companies is to go onto Yahoo Finance and search the company's ticker symbol. Under the current price of the stock and other pertinent information there is a list of links with articles related to that company. You can do this too by going online and finding articles related to the stocks you own. This is a great way to follow the companies in which you own shares and remain "in the loop" regarding each company's current news.

In addition to researching articles online, you can sometimes find very good ones in printed newspapers and magazines. You can also look up all the statistics about your stocks in the newspaper as well. The articles in the newspapers can give you insights into the future plans of the different companies you own, and also alert you to any current problems a company might need to address or successes it might have had that could affect its profitability.

Tracking quarterly earnings

Another excellent way to really understand the performance of the stocks you own is to closely track the quarterly earnings reported by the company. Quarterly earnings numbers are announced just four times a year (hence the term quarterly), but those numbers can provide information that's essential to predicting the company's future worth. You can look online to find out the next date that the company in which you have stock will release its quarterly earnings information. How your company did during the quarter in comparison to investors', and the company's own, predictions will usually have an immediate effect on the stock price. For instance, if the company beat expectations for their quarterly earnings then the stock's price will likely go up, but if they announce earnings that are less than expected, then the price will probably go down. Remember though, just because a company has a bad quarter does not mean that it won't end the fiscal year with better-than-expected earnings.

Why is it important to keep track of your stocks?

It is very important that you follow your stocks and take an interest in how each company in which you own stock is doing. The performance of a company is generally reflected in its stock price, so if you do not understand a company's performance, you may end up surprised by a change in stock price. This could be a good surprise, but it could also be a very bad surprise. For this reason, it's important that you try to stay updated on the current events and news surrounding a company in which you own stock so you don't miss events that could affect the stock's price. Think about it this way: you own a part of that company, so you'll want to understand how and what your company is doing, and probably also to research and think about different factors that might affect its continuing profitability.

> *"Good luck with future investing and remember what you learned!"*

GLOSSARY

Assets
A resource owned by a company for the future benefit to their business

Central auction market
A market where buyers and sellers make simultaneous offers on a stock which determines its price

Earnings
The profit a company produces in a certain time period; usually released by the company each quarter (3 months)

Exchange traded funds (ETF's)
A security that follows an index or a basket of assets and is traded like a stock

Indexes
A group of securities which represent a specific market or a part of it

Initial public offering (IPO)
The first sale of stock by a private company to the public

Listing standards
Requirements made by stock exchanges that must be fulfilled by companies in order to sell company stock on a specific exchange

Public companies
Companies that offer shares of their business to the public on at least one stock exchange

Security
A financial position that demonstrates ownership of a specific stock or bond

Shares
A unit of a stock which can be sold individually; an investor may own thousands of shares of stock of a single company

Stock exchanges
A marketplace or platform where securities are traded between companies and the public

Shareholders
    A person, company, or any other institution that owns at least one share of a stock

Volatile
    When a stock is very unpredictable

REFERENCES

www.investopedia.com

The Stock Market by Orli Zuravicky

The Bull and the Bear by Avelyn Davidson

Made in the USA
San Bernardino, CA
04 June 2018